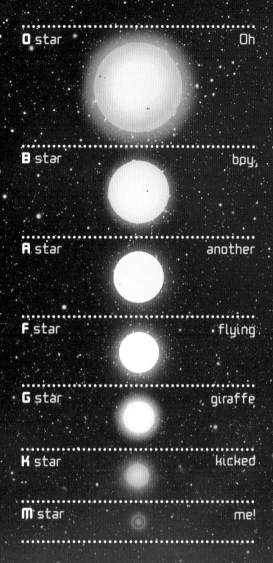

O star   Oh

B star   bpy,

A star   another

F star   flying

G star   giraffe

K star   kicked

M star   me!

Astronomers classify stars according to their temperature and size. The hottest stars are the biggest and glow bright blue. The coolest and smallest stars glow a dim red. In between they glow white, yellow, and orange. An easy way to remember their order is by using the saying above. The stars you see above are called main sequence stars. This is their normal appearance throughout most of their lifetime. In the last stages of their life, except for the tiny M stars, all these stars swell up into red giants. O, B, and A stars eventually explode as supernovae, while F, G, and K stars shrink down from red giants to white dwarfs, slowly cooling over time until they eventually grow cold and die.

Red Giant

White Dwarf

NATIONAL GEOGRAPHIC
KID'S

SUPER STARS

THE BIGGEST, HOTTEST, BRIGHTEST, MOST EXPLOSIVE STARS IN THE MILKY WAY

BY DAVID A. AGUILAR

NATIONAL GEOGRAPHIC
WASHINGTON, D.C.

This book is dedicated to these four rising SUPER STARS:
Bree, Aiden, Penelope, and Taylor (aka "Satellite Girl")

PUBLISHED BY THE NATIONAL GEOGRAPHIC SOCIETY

John M. Fahey, Jr.,
President & Chief Executive Officer

Gilbert M. Grosvenor,
Chairman of the Board

Tim T. Kelly,
President, Global Media Group

John Q. Griffin,
Executive Vice President;
President, Publishing

Nina D. Hoffman,
Executive Vice President;
President, Book Publishing Group

Melina Gerosa Bellows,
Executive Vice President,
Children's Publishing

PREPARED BY THE BOOK DIVISION

Nancy Laties Feresten,
Vice President, Editor in Chief,
Children's Books

Jonathan Halling,
Design Director,
Children's Publishing

Jennifer Emmett,
Executive Editor, Reference &
Solo Titles, Children's Books

Carl Mehler,
Director of Maps

R. Gary Colbert,
Production Director

Jennifer A. Thornton,
Managing Editor

STAFF FOR THIS BOOK

Rebecca Baines,
Project Editor

David M. Seager,
Art Director

Lori Epstein,
Illustrations Editor

Grace Hill,
Associate Managing Editor

Kate Olesin,
Editorial Assistant

Lewis R. Bassford,
Production Manager

Susan Borke,
Legal and Business Affairs

Manufacturing and Quality Management

Christopher A. Liedel,
Chief Financial Officer

Phillip L. Schlosser,
Vice President

Chris Brown,
Technical Director

Nicole Elliott, Rachel Faulise,
Managers

The National Geographic Society is one of the world's largest nonprofit scientific and educational organizations. Founded in 1888 to "increase and diffuse geographic knowledge," the Society works to inspire people to care about the planet. It reaches more than 325 million people worldwide each month through its official journal, *National Geographic,* and other magazines; National Geographic Channel; television documentaries; music; radio; films; books; DVDs; maps; exhibitions; school publishing programs; interactive media; and merchandise. National Geographic has funded more than 9,000 scientific research, conservation and exploration projects and supports an education program combating geographic illiteracy. For more information, visit nationalgeographic.com.

For more information, please call 1-800-NGS LINE (647-5463) or write to the following address:

National Geographic Society
1145 17th Street N.W.
Washington, D.C. 20036-4688 U.S.A.

Visit us online at www.nationalgeographic. com/books

For librarians and teachers:
www.ngchildrensbooks.org

More for kids from National Geographic:
kids.nationalgeographic.com

For information about special discounts for bulk purchases, please contact National Geographic Books Special Sales: ngspecsales@ngs.org

For rights or permissions inquiries, please contact National Geographic Books Subsidiary Rights: ngbookrights@ngs.org

Library of Congress Cataloging-in-Publication Data

Aguilar, David A.
Super stars: the biggest, hottest, brightest, and most explosive stars in the Milky Way / by David A. Aguilar.
    p. cm.
Includes bibliographical references and index.
ISBN 978-1-4263-0601-3 (hardcover : alk. paper)
— ISBN 978-1-4263-0602-0 (lib. bdg. : alk. paper)
1. Supergiant stars—Juvenile literature. 2. Supermassive stars—Juvenile literature. 3. Stars, Brightest—Juvenile literature. I. Title.
QB843.S9A48 2010
523.8'8—dc22

2009037124

Printed in China
10/RRDS/1

ILLUSTRATION CREDITS

All illustrations by David A. Aguilar, unless otherwise noted below:

Ken Crawford: 20 bottom; Rob Gendler: 13 bottom, 30 bottom, 42 top left, 43 top left; NASA: 25 bottom; David M. Seager; 9 top, 10 top, 13 top, 14 top, 17 top, 18 top, 21 top, 21 center, 22 top, 22 center, 25 top, 29 top, 29 center, 30 top, 35 top, 35 center, 36 top, 36 center, 39 top, 42 top, 43 top, 44 top, 45 top; Shutterstock: 47 all

CONTENTS

LIFE CYCLE OF STARS

STEP 1
NEBULA

swirling dust
and gases

The Hubble Space Telescope, launched in 1990, has returned thousands of gorgeous images of brilliant red dust clouds that stretch light-years across space. So you might argue that the favorite color of the universe is red. But look at it another way, and you can see that the favorite color of the cosmos is actually green! Today, everybody talks about "going green" by recycling natural resources.

STEP 3
for Sun-like
Stars:
RED GIANT

STEP 2
for Small
Stars:
OUR SUN

STEP 3
for the Largest Stars:
RED SUPER GIANT

STEP 2
for Large
Stars:
BLUE GIANT

6

Guess what? The universe has been recycling since the very beginning of time. All stars, planets, moons, comets, and everything else in the universe, including you and me, are products of this fantastic recycling program. Stars and planets form from gas and dust clouds left over from earlier dying stars. When material within these gas clouds is drawn together by gravity, it swirls around and forms new stars and solar systems.

Eventually, when stars run out of fuel, they swell up and become red giants. Smaller stars collapse, puffing out nebular bubbles that supply fresh new materials for future star formation. Giant stars explode as supernovae, combining lighter elements like the gases hydrogen and helium into new heavier elements like the iron and sodium found in our bodies. These elements mix with gas and dust from other dying stars to make new stars and planets. Scientists have found that each human being contains about one teaspoon of heavy elements that were produced in two separate star deaths. That means everything we see around us, including you and your friends and family, has been recycled twice. Green is not just a great color—it's how our universe works!

CONSTELLATIONS
Constellations are groups of stars that form a pattern in the sky. To astronomers, constellations are like countries on a map. They are used to refer to the location of stars or other objects in space. Many of the 88 recognized constellations came from the ancient Greeks. They looked at these star patterns in the northern sky and used them to tell stories about gods and goddesses as well as wonderful mythical creatures like flying horses and giant scorpions. In this book, you can find each star's constellation listed at the top of the page, underneath the star's name. Use the charts on pages 42–45 as your guide to the sky!

STEP 4
for Sun-like Stars:
PLANETARY NEBULA

STEP 5
for Sun-like Stars:
WHITE DWARF
After this, they grow dark and disappear.

STEP 4
for Large Stars:
SUPERNOVA

STEP 5
for Large Stars:
NEUTRON STAR

STEP 5
for Really Huge Stars:
BLACK HOLE

GLOBULAR CLUSTERS

NAME OMEGA CENTAURI
CONSTELLATION Centaurus
DISTANCE FROM EARTH 15,890 light-years
VISIBILITY Telescope
STAR CHART Page 45

THE DEAD ZONE

The oldest stars in the universe shine down on us every night. They are tightly packed together in spherical groups called globular clusters that move around the edges of galaxies. Because life-supporting elements like iron, copper, and calcium are missing from these stars, they are called the dead zones of space. These balls of stars are very important to astronomers. Each cluster is at least 12 billion years old, so scientists can study them to find out what the early universe was like. In the beginning, there were thousands of them in the neighborhood of our galaxy. Over time collisions have destroyed or combined most of them into the fewer than 150 clusters that today form a halo around the Milky Way. The most magnificent of all these ancient clusters is Omega Centauri, which contains over 10 million stars and looks as big in our sky as the full moon, even though it is much farther away. It is one of the most beautiful objects you can see in a telescope.

DID YOU KNOW?

IN GLOBULAR CLUSTERS, THE STARS ARE SO CLOSE TOGETHER, COLLISIONS AND NEAR MISSES ARE QUITE COMMON.

Buzzing around the edge of our galaxy like a swarm of bees almost 150 light-years wide, Omega Centauri (left) stands out as the largest and brightest of the globular clusters surrounding the Milky Way.

If we could stand on a world hidden inside Omega Centauri, the sky would be illuminated by millions of brilliant stars packed so tightly together it would be impossible to see beyond them and easy to forget the rest of the universe existed.

DIFFUSE NEBULAE

NAME ORION NEBULA
CONSTELLATION Orion
DISTANCE FROM EARTH 1,500 light-years
VISIBILITY Binoculars/Telescope
STAR CHART Pages 43/44

COSMIC DAY CARE

On those cold, clear December nights, as the constellation Orion (the Hunter) lifts his shield toward the neighboring constellation Taurus (the Bull), look closely and you will see a smudge of light that hangs down from the hunter's belt. Legend says it is his sword, but astronomers know it's actually a magnificent star factory called the Great Nebula in Orion. It is one of many clouds of gas and dust called diffuse nebulae (nebula means "cloud" in Greek), where new stars blaze into life. Inside a nebula, gas and dust collected from earlier supernova explosions and clumps of material floating through space are drawn together. They pack more and more tightly until they eventually ignite and become stars lighting the surrounding nebula, making it glow like a billboard. Covering an area almost four full moons in size, the Orion Nebula is the brightest stellar nursery visible from Earth.

DID YOU KNOW?

TO MANY OBSERVERS, THE ORION NEBULA LOOKS LIKE A MANTA RAY SWIMMING IN SPACE.

This infant star (just a few million years old) inside the Orion Nebula has a dust ring around it that will eventually form planets. The Hubble Space Telescope has photographed more than 150 new solar systems forming inside the Orion Nebula.

Inside the Great Nebula in Orion four bright stars form a group called the Trapezium (right), because it resembles a trapeze in the circus. These baby stars began shining a few hundred million years ago. The objects that look like tadpoles are newly forming stars surrounded by dust.

OPEN STAR CLUSTERS

NAME THE PLEIADES
CONSTELLATION Taurus
DISTANCE FROM EARTH 440 light-years
VISIBILITY Naked eye/Binoculars
STAR CHART Pages 43/44

DIAMONDS IN THE SKY

The Pleiades (PLEE-UH-DEEZ), or Seven Sisters, is the brightest and newest star cluster in our sky. You can easily see it with your naked eyes, but your best view is through binoculars. Open star clusters are young stars that have just emerged from stellar nurseries like the Orion Nebula (pages 10-11). Our Sun was part of an open star cluster more than 4 billion years ago. As the baby stars began shining and drifting apart, their solar winds blasted away the clouds of the remaining nebula, leaving our Sun by itself. But the Pleiades are so young that bits of their cloudy nebula still form halos around them. The light from these stars travels 440 years to get to us, so the starlight we see from them tonight left the Pleiades about the year 1570. This was shortly after Shakespeare was born and about 40 years before Galileo first turned his telescope to the heavens.

DID YOU KNOW?

WHEN THE EARLY DINOSAURS WALKED ON EARTH, THE PLEIADES HADN'T BEEN BORN YET.

Seen here from an imagined alien world, the Pleiades (left) blaze like rich jewels down upon giant alien creatures. Because life may be so strange on other worlds, we can let our imagination run wild.

The Double cluster in Perseus is another magnificent example of new open star clusters. Born next to each other a few million years ago, they are best viewed in amateur-size telescopes. These clusters are located about 7,000 light-years away.

BROWN DWARFS

NAME **TEIDE 1**

CONSTELLATION Taurus

DISTANCE FROM EARTH 400 light-years

VISIBILITY Observatory

STAR CHART Page 43

FAILURE IS AN OPTION

Forget about it! Everybody fails at something in their lifetime. Imagine how frustrating it must be for brown dwarfs. They are born in star nurseries, but while most baby stars collect enough matter to pull tightly together and start shining, others just don't. They glow a dark red color, shining just brightly enough for astronomers to see them with infrared telescopes. After a few million years, their dull glow begins to fade, and they grow dimmer and dimmer until their fires go out and they disappear from view. Even though brown dwarfs start life like stars, they don't officially count because they never truly shine. In many ways they are a lot like gas giant planets. Some astronomers think they are the missing link between gas giant planets and M stars.

Brown dwarf   Jupiter

DID YOU KNOW?

ALL BROWN DWARFS ARE JUST A LITTLE BIT BIGGER THAN JUPITER!

The Milky Way is filled with millions of brown dwarfs that we cannot see. They may be as common as planets. However, because they send out so little heat and light, they quickly fade from view.

Looking like a glowing coal, Teide 1 (right) is a young stellar wannabe, the first brown dwarf ever discovered. If there are planets orbiting around it, as shown here, it is unlikely any life exists on these dark dusty worlds because the light and heat coming from Teide 1 is too weak.

MULTIPLE STARS

NAME BETA LYRAE
CONSTELLATION Lyra
DISTANCE FROM EARTH 882 light-years
VISIBILITY Telescope
STAR CHART Page 42

A FAMILY AFFAIR

Look up into the sky tonight, and imagine this: More than one-third of all the stars you see are actually multiple star systems, meaning they are made up of two or more stars. Sunsets on worlds circling these stars would look like Luke Skywalker's home planet Tatooine, where there are two giant suns in the sky. When stars form in nebular clouds like the Orion Nebula, dense regions may produce stars very near to each other.

In fact, some may be so close that gravity locks them together forever. They are held into one tight family. One of the weirdest of these multiple systems is the triple star system Beta Lyrae. Two of the stars are so close together that their atmospheres trade gas and dust. As this moving stream flows from one star to the other, some of it is thrown out into an ever widening dusty spiral surrounding both stars.

Seen from an imaginary world, two of the stars in Beta Lyrae (left) are separated by less than 30 million miles, or the distance between Mercury and our Sun. Dust flows from these two egg-shaped stars at an amazing speed of 180 million miles a second.

Not all multiple stars are white in color. Albireo, in the constellation Cygnus (the Swan), is one of the most stunning double stars ever seen in an amateur telescope. One star is sparkling aquamarine blue and the other is radiant yellow-gold.

ECLIPSING STARS

WELCOME TO THE STARS

NAME **ALGOL**
CONSTELLATION Perseus
DISTANCE FROM EARTH 94 light-years
VISIBILITY Naked eye
STAR CHART Pages 42/44

THE WINKING DEMON

Look up tonight and you just might see the constellation Perseus holding up the head of the snake-haired Gorgon woman named Medusa. Then again, unless you are an ancient Greek, you may miss it completely. However, you can still see the star that Greek poets thought was the remains of the Gorgon's head. Its name is Algol, the winking demon star. It sounds like a monster right out of a Saturday morning cartoon. Algol is a triple star system where, like Beta Lyrae (pages 16-17), two of the stars are very close together and the third is farther away. The two close stars orbit each other so that every three days the dimmer one blocks the light from the brighter one. When that happens, Algol looks dimmer to us. When they move apart, Algol looks brighter. Many ancient cultures gave this ominous winking star names meaning ogre, demon, ghost, ghoul, or devil's head.

DID YOU KNOW?

THE NAME ALGOL COMES FROM THE ARABIC WORDS AL GHUL, MEANING "THE DEMON."

Viewed at night from a big open space like the Sahara desert, Algol changes from being a very bright star to almost disappearing from view every three days. Do you think it looks like the evil eye of a monster looking back at you?

The companion stars that make up Algol (right) trade stellar material back and forth. When the orange star passes in front of the brighter blue star, the light suddenly drops by 70 percent.

NEUTRON STARS

NAME XTE J1739-285
CONSTELLATION Ophiuchus
DISTANCE FROM EARTH 39,000 light-years
VISIBILITY Observatory
STAR CHART Pages 42/45

FASTEST SPINNING STAR

From planets to asteroids, we know almost everything in space spins. Earth takes about 24 hours to spin once. Jupiter takes 10 hours, fast enough that it bulges slightly in the middle. Our Sun rotates approximately once every 25 days. But the one star in the Milky Way that has smashed the speed record for spinning is the neutron star XTE J1739-285. In the universe, there are unusual stars, bizarre stars, and then there are neutron stars. These are the corpses of giant stars that have exploded as supernovae. XTE J1739-285 spins faster than astronomers thought any star was capable of spinning without tearing itself apart. This tiny white star roughly six miles in diameter spins an unbelievable 1,122 times per second or 40 times faster than the propeller on an airplane. It is the fastest spinning star we know of in the Milky Way.

DID YOU KNOW?

NEUTRON STARS ARE SO DENSE, ONE SPOONFUL CAN WEIGH AS MUCH AS A SCHOOL BUS.

XTE J1739-285 (left), seen in this painting, is the last remains of a rapidly spinning dying star that still blasts x-rays into space. It was detected by the Chandra X-Ray Space Telescope.

Big stars can spin fast, too. Achernar, a blue giant in the constellation Eridanius, spins nearly 100 times faster than our Sun. Its spin speed makes it the flattest star in the Milky Way.

PULSARS

NAME B1508+55
CONSTELLATION Currently in Draco
DISTANCE FROM EARTH 7,700 light-years
VISIBILITY Observatory
STAR CHART Pages 42/43

LIGHTHOUSES IN THE SKY

The lighthouse that was built in the third century B.C. in Alexandria, Egypt, is listed as one of the Seven Wonders of the Ancient World. A mirror would reflect the light from a fire set on the stone floor to another mirror 400 feet up at the very top. When the light hit the top mirror, it then bounced out over the harbor. As spectacular as this must have been to the ancient Greeks, imagine a cosmic lighthouse capable of sending light thousands of light-years across space while spinning at the amazing rate of 716 times a second! This fastest spinning pulsar, named B1508+55, is a highly magnetized, rotating neutron star that sends out a beam of light as it spins. It is speeding through the Milky Way at the amazing rate of 670 miles a second. That's 37,000 times faster than your parents drive down the interstate. Scientists believe that around 2.5 million years ago a supernova blasted B1508+55 away from its home somewhere near the constellation Cygnus (the Swan). It is traveling so fast that this cosmic lighthouse will eventually leave our galaxy to roam the universe alone.

In 1967, astronomers detected a strange pulsing radio signal from the Crab Nebula. It blinked on and off about once every second. Some astronomers joked it must be LGM signals, or messages from little green men. It turned out to be the first discovery of a pulsar.

The pulsar B1508+55 (right) sends out two beacons of light, seen here sweeping past an alien planet. Unlike lighthouses back on Earth, this cosmic beacon is spinning at the astounding rate of 716 times per second.

G STARS

NOT YOUR AVERAGE STAR

Our Sun is a yellow G star. Compared to other stars, it is considered a medium size, middle-aged, unremarkable star. Of course to us it has always been special. It is the shining ball of light that burns 93 million miles away and makes life on Earth possible. And recent discoveries reveal it's special in other ways as well. When we look for Earth-like planets around distant stars, we pick stars similar to our Sun because they have long life spans of up to 15 billion years, which is plenty of time for life to develop. Even better, where some stars' energy output changes wildly, G stars are stable energy producers. So how many Sun-like stars are in the Milky Way? Very few it seems, less than 2.5 percent. This makes the nearest star to the Earth not so common after all.

DID YOU KNOW?

FIVE BILLION YEARS FROM NOW, OUR SUN WILL BECOME A RED GIANT STAR.

The sunlight that is currently shining on Earth, the International Space Station, and the moon (left), was generated in the Sun's core 50 million years ago. After working its way to the surface, it took another 8.3 minutes to travel through space and reach us here on Earth.

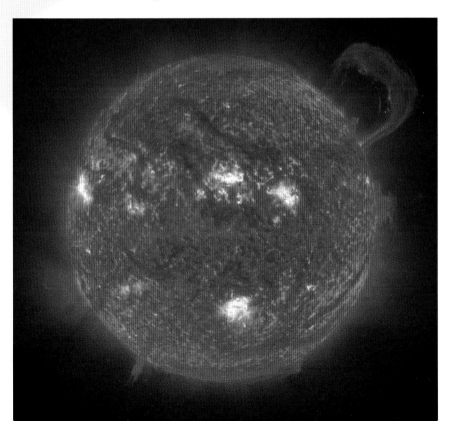

This giant solar flare erupting off the surface of the Sun stretches almost a quarter of a million miles into space. Just one huge flare like this can unleash enough energy to supply all the power needed by the world for about five years.

25

Any day now, astronomers may discover the first Earth-like planet circling around a distant star. In the meantime, they have found something just as exciting. Gliese (GLEE-zee) 581 is a red dwarf star one-third the size of our Sun. Red dwarf stars are smaller and cooler than our Sun. They are the most common type of star in the universe. Circling around Gliese 581 are four planets named b, c, d, and e. Planet d orbits at just the right distance for liquid water—and maybe life—to exist on it.

This planet is too large to be a rocky planet like Earth. Instead, it may be a water world with mountaintops sticking out of one gigantic ocean. Because red dwarfs radiate infrared light (heat) rather than the rainbow of colors we see from our Sun, planet d would look dark to us. But if life-forms exist there, they would have developed infrared vision. They would see colors based on how hot or cool things are. Cold rocks could look blue, while glowing nebulae might look red in a fiery sky.

Near the red dwarf star Gliese 581, planet d is the large planet in the foreground, possibly covered in water and orbited by a moon. Planet c glows bright white like Venus and planet b has a comet tail. Planet e is not visible in this image as it is so close to Gliese 581, it is lost in the glare of the star.

LIFE-GIVING STARS

NAME MIRA
CONSTELLATION Cetus
DISTANCE FROM EARTH 420 light-years
VISIBILITY Naked eye
STAR CHART Pages 43/ 44

SEEDING THE UNIVERSE

Mira is a red giant star in the last stages of its life. A variable star, it pulses like a beating heart as it changes in size from 400 times the diameter of the Sun to 500 times the diameter of the Sun over a period of 331 days. In fact, it is the brightest and most studied variable star in our sky. And it's fast, too, racing along at almost 300,000 miles an hour through the constellation Cetus. But Mira has something more amazing still—a comet-like tail trailing 13 light-years, or 20,000 times the distance between the Sun and Pluto, behind it, leaving a trail of complex chemicals in its wake. It is sometimes called the "Johnny Appleseed star" because much like Johnny Appleseed planted future apple trees all over the early American frontier, Mira is seeding the universe with gas and dust that may someday sprout new stars and planets.

DID YOU KNOW?

THE CARBON IN OUR MUSCLES AND THE OXYGEN WE BREATHE CAME FROM RED GIANT STARS LIKE MIRA.

The egg-shaped red giant star Mira (left), whose name means "the wonderful," passes by a Neptune-size world where green auroras ripple across the polar night skies. Mira has a magnificent comet-like tail trailing almost 80 trillion miles behind it.

Besides comet tails, there are other ways dying stars help seed the universe. The Bubble Nebula, located 7,100 light-years from Earth, is a cast-off teardrop of gas and dust shed by the massive star buried deep inside it.

29

PLANETARY NEBULAE

NAME GHOST OF JUPITER
CONSTELLATION Hydra
DISTANCE FROM EARTH 1,400 light-years
VISIBILITY Telescope
STAR CHART Page 44

COSMIC TOMBSTONES

Since the beginning of recorded time, historians have discovered tombstones marking the graves of our ancestors. Just like these ancient grave markers, medium-size stars like our Sun leave cosmic tombstones behind. As Sun-like stars run out of fuel, they swell up and transform into red giant stars. In the last moments before shrinking down into white dwarfs, they puff out layers of gas called planetary nebulae. Early astronomers thought they looked like ghostly versions of gas giant planets such as Neptune and Jupiter, and the name is derived from this eerie appearance. These glowing shells only last a few thousand years before fading away. No planetary nebula is visible from Earth with the naked eye. However, many of them, including the Ghost of Jupiter (officially named NGC 3242), are spectacular when viewed through a small telescope.

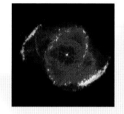

DID YOU KNOW?

THE CAT'S EYE NEBULA IN THE CONSTELLATION DRACO LOOKS LIKE A ROSE TO MANY OBSERVERS.

The Dumbbell Nebula, or M27, was the first planetary nebula ever discovered. Located in the constellation Vulpecula (near Cygnus), it is the brightest planetary nebula in the night sky and easily visible in a small telescope.

The Ghost of Jupiter, or NGC 3242 (right), with the Milky Way galaxy in the background, is the glowing remains of the passing of an ancient Sun-like star. It is one of 3,000 planetary nebulae known to exist in our galaxy.

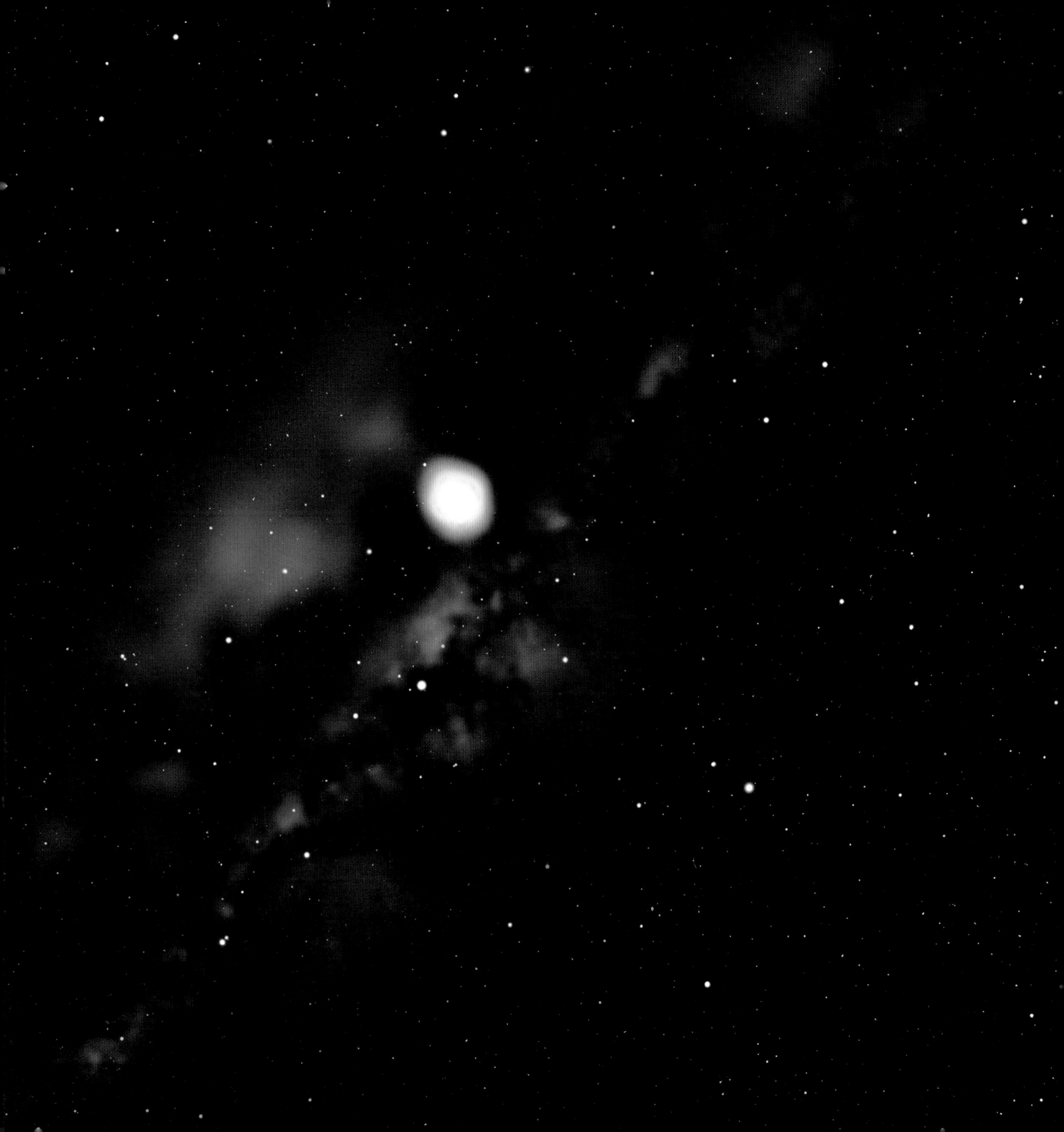

In addition to cosmic tombstones, planetary nebulae have also been called the butterflies of the universe because of their bright colors, wild shapes, and short lifetimes. Visible for only a few thousand years, their shapes and colors are the result of many factors, including how fast the star was spinning before the red giant phase collapsed, if there was another star or giant planet nearby to pull on it, and the strength of the star's magnetic field. All these factors determine what type of cosmic butterfly will float through space.

The Eskimo Nebula (1) looks like an Eskimo; M2–9 (2) is rapidly spinning with jets shooting out; Abel 39 (3) is like a round soap bubble; M57 (4) is shaped like a donut; the red Hourglass Nebula (5), with the blue, oxygen-rich "eye," has two giant clouds of gas shaped like soup bowls shooting out in opposite directions; and IC418 (6) has gas clouds that look like ocean waves.

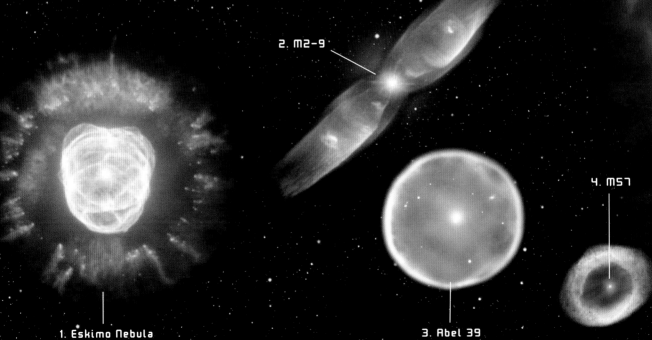

2. M2–9

4. M57

1. Eskimo Nebula

3. Abel 39

6 . IC418

5. Hourglass Nebula

SUPERNOVAE

BOOM! THERE GOES THE NEIGHBORHOOD

DID YOU KNOW?

THE BIGGEST AND BRIGHTEST SUPERNOVA MOST RECENTLY VIEWED FROM EARTH OCCURRED IN 1987.

Eta Carinae (left) experienced a false supernova explosion 150 years ago, when it suddenly became the brightest star in the southern sky. This outburst produced two billowing clouds of gas with enough material to make at least two new solar systems with suns like our own.

Volcanologists are scientists who observe volcanoes to try and predict when they will erupt. Seismologists record small tremors in the earth for warnings of violent earthquakes to come. Astrophysicists search for supernovae, the biggest explosions in the universe. Supernovae occur when normal stars that are 8 to 20 times the size of our Sun run out of fuel to burn and swell up into massive red giants. Near the end of their lives, red giants collapse, resulting in huge explosions! Located 7,500 light-years away from Earth, the red giant Eta Carinae is the next best candidate to become a supernova. This star is so big (approximately 180 times the size of our Sun) that when it blows, it will shine so brightly we will be able to see it in the daytime. For several months, the night sky will radiate a bluish glow strong enough to read by. Luckily, Eta Carinae is tilted 45 degrees away from us so the deadly gamma radiation and high-energy outbursts of its supernova will miss Earth. We will be spared any damage and be treated to the biggest fireworks show the universe has to offer.

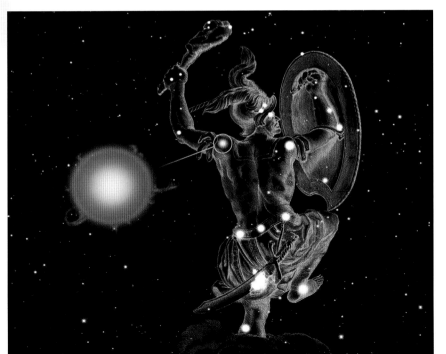

Another candidate to become a supernova is the red giant star Betelgeuse, located at the shoulder of Orion (the Hunter). If it flared up tomorrow night, it would mean the blast actually occurred 600 years ago, a few years before Christopher Columbus set sail for the New World.

HYPERGIANTS

GREAT BALLS OF FIRE

From supersize meals to monster trucks, it seems like everybody today likes things big. So, we should especially be interested in the hypergiant star VY Canis Major. It is the biggest known star in the Milky Way. A red giant is the last phase of a star's life, when it balloons up to hundreds of times its normal size and turns orange-red in color. VY Canis Major is a monster red supergiant star so big, if we switched it with our Sun, its diameter would be bigger than the orbit of Saturn. Everything inside, including Jupiter and all the inner planets, would be burned to cinders. Less than a million years ago, it started out as a rare gigantic O star 4,900 light-years away from Earth. Now it is a monster senior citizen in the last stages of its life.

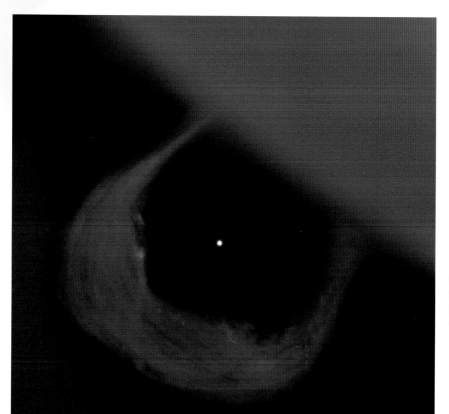

VY Canis Major (right) fills the sky of a burned out planet. However, the best is yet to come. Soon, it will run out of fuel and collapse, producing either the most spectacular supernova ever seen or a giant black hole.

DID YOU KNOW?

VY CANIS MAJOR IS SO BIG THAT ALMOST A MILLION STARS LIKE OUR SUN COULD FIT INSIDE IT.

So just how big is this monster star? The tiny white dot you see between the star and a solar flare is our Sun. Traveling in a spaceship at the speed of light, it would take less than 5 seconds to travel across the face of our Sun and 2.5 hours to travel across the face of VY Canis Major.

BLACK HOLES

NAME SAGITTARIUS A
CONSTELLATION behind Sagittarius
DISTANCE FROM EARTH 28,000 light-years
VISIBILITY Observatory
STAR CHART Page 45

COSMIC VACUUM CLEANERS

A black hole really *is* a hole in space, where no light can escape because the gravity is too strong. Black holes are the mystery spots where planets and stars disappear and never come out. They form when giant stars collapse, leaving a "cosmic vacuum cleaner" behind that pulls in anything that gets near it. Like shoes, they come in different sizes. Small ones weigh about three times the weight of the Sun. Monster black holes weigh 4 million times the weight of the Sun and are found at the centers of galaxies. The black hole at the center of the Milky Way is called Sagittarius A. You can't see it because it's hidden behind thick dust clouds located between us and it. Recently, radio astronomers detected a giant flare up from this monster when it snacked on something the size of a planet. Fortunately Earth is located a very distant 28,000 light-years away, so it will never become dinner!

DID YOU KNOW?

FALLING INTO A BLACK HOLE WOULD STRETCH THE ATOMS IN YOUR BODY UNTIL NOTHING RECOGNIZABLE WAS LEFT.

In this artist rendering, gas and dust from a yellow star are pulled into the black hole Sagittarius A (left), forming a disk shape around it. Soon, the star will spiral in and disappear forever.

Small, rogue black holes may roam the Milky Way, threatening to swallow up anything that gets in their way. These relics from the past formed when our galaxy was quite young and the first stars began to die. Don't worry, they're too far away to ever reach us.

39

Someday, we are going to find a way to travel to the stars. When we do, it will open up the exploration of space and possible encounters with new forms of alien life. So where do we begin our star quest? The first choice will be Alpha Centauri—the nearest star system to the Sun. Located 4.3 light-years away, Alpha Centauri is a triple star system of two remarkably Sun-like stars, Alpha Centauri A and B, locked in orbit around each other, and a small red dwarf star named Proxima Centauri.

Although no gas giant planets have been detected orbiting these stars, smaller rocky planets may exist, hidden by the glare. Slightly older than our Sun, Alpha Centauri A and B are exciting places to begin our search for a new home away from home.

In the not—too—distant future, a starship like this may arrive at Alpha Centauri after completing a 40—year journey from Earth to explore planets that may exist there. To the left, orange—colored Alpha Centauri B glows brightly while the red dwarf Proxima Centauri is barely visible on this page to the left of Alpha Centauri A.

NORTH

2 DUMBBELL NEBULA

3 M13 GLOBULAR CLUSTER

WE LOOK TO THE STARS

Perseus
Algol
Double Cluster
Cassiopeia
Ursa Major
Andromeda
Bubble Nebula
Cepheus
Ursa Minor
Draco
B1508+55
Pegasus
Pisces
Cygnus
Hercules
Boötes
Virgo
4
Lyra
3
Corona Borealis
2 1
Delphinus
Aquilla
Ophiuchus
Gliese 581
Aquarius
Libra
XTE J-1739
Capricornus
Sagittarius
Scorpio

EAST

WEST

ALBIREO

1

NORTHERN HEMISPHERE ★ SUMMER/FALL

EPSILON LYRAE 4

42

SOUTH

2 ORION NEBULA

3 PLEIADES

WE LOOK TO THE STARS

Draco

81508+55

Cepheus

Bubble
Nebula

Ursa
Minor

Cassiopeia

Andromeda

Boötes

Double
Cluster

Perseus

Algol

Ursa
Major

Aries

Virgo

Auriga

Gemini

4

3

Taurus

Leo

Cancer

Crab Nebula

1

Orion

Mira

Crater

Canis
Minor

2

Cetus

Hydra

Canis
Major

EAST

WEST

BETELGEUSE

1

TEIDE 1

4

NORTHERN HEMISPHERE ★ WINTER/SPRING

2 GHOST OF JUPITER

3 PLEIADES

WELCOME TO THE STARS

Auriga

Algol

Perseus

Leo

Gemini

Crab Nebula

Taurus

Cancer

3

Aries

Canis Minor

Orion

1

Monoceros

Sextans

Lepus

Mira

4

Canis Major

Crater

2

Pyxis

Eridanus

Corvus

Vela

Carina

Cetus

Hydra

Crux

Centaurus

EAST

WEST

ORION NEBULA

1

SOUTHERN HEMISPHERE ★ SUMMER/FALL VY CANIS MAJOR 4

44

WELCOME TO THE STARS

2 ALPHA CENTAURI

3 OMEGA CENTAURI

EAST

WEST

Cygnus

Lyra

Hercules

Corona Borealis

Boötes

Aquilla

Delphinus

Ophiuchus

Virgo

Gliese 581

XTE J-1739

Libra

1

Capricornus

Scorpio

Lupus

Corvus

Sagittarius

Centaurus

Crater

Aquarius

2

3

Hydra

Piscis Austrinus

Crux

4

Vela

Carina

SAGITTARIUS A

ETA CARINAE 4

1

GLOSSARY

CONSTELLATION: A pattern of stars identified with an ancient god, goddess, or animal; also an area of sky with one of these star patterns.

ECLIPSE: When one celestial object is blocked from view in the sky by another celestial object.

ELEMENTS: The basic building blocks of all matter.

EXTRATERRESTRIAL LIFE: Life that might exist elsewhere beyond the Earth.

GALAXY: A grouping of stars and planets held together by gravity. Earth is in the Milky Way galaxy.

GAS GIANT: A large planet that is primarily comprised of swirling gases. In our solar system, Jupiter, Saturn, Uranus, and Neptune are all gas giants.

HUBBLE SPACE TELESCOPE: A giant space telescope that was sent into orbit aboard the space shuttle in 1990. It is the most important research tool in space.

INFRARED: Invisible radiation wavelengths of light, just beyond red in the visible spectrum. We feel infrared as heat.

INTERNATIONAL SPACE STATION: A research facility in Earth orbit shared by the U.S., Japan, Russia, Canada, and Europe.

LIGHT-YEAR: The distance light can travel in one year (5.9 trillion miles).

NEBULA/NEBULAR CLOUD: A cloud of interstellar gas and dust.

NEUTRON STAR: The remains left behind when a star explodes as a supernova.

PLANET: A round object that orbits a star and does not create its own light.

ROCKY PLANET: Also known as a terrestrial planet, rocky planets have metallic cores and a firm surface. In our solar system, Mercury, Venus, Earth, and Mars are all rocky planets.

SOLAR FLARE: A sudden violent explosion of energy that occurs in the Sun's atmosphere near a sunspot.

STAR: A bright celestial object that gives off light by energy produced in its core.

SUPERNOVA: An explosion that occurs when a massive red giant collapses.

UNIVERSE: Everything there is.

X-RAY: A type of highly energetic particles that can pass through our skin.

COMPOSITION OF OUR SUN

Our Sun's photosphere—what we see from Earth—is composed of about 74% hydrogen and 25% helium gas with tiny amounts of other things like iron, carbon, oxygen, and sulfur. In the center of the Sun is the hydrogen-dense core. It is here that a process called nuclear fusion takes two simple atoms of hydrogen and smashes them together, forming a new helium atom. The little extra energy created by this action produces the heat and light we experience during the day. Sometimes, as that energy radiates out toward the photosphere of the Sun, darker sunspots appear. From these sunspots, loops, or solar flares, of super hot gases shoot out, sending huge amounts of extra energy through space. Besides disrupting satellite communications, they also accentuate the beautiful colored aurora borealis and aurora australis, or northern and southern lights, that we see on Earth.

THE SPEED OF LIGHT

Light travels at a speed of 186,282 miles a second. That means if you could shine a flashlight around Earth, the beam would circle the globe 8 times in one second. Because light travels so fast, astronomers use it to describe the distance of stars and galaxies across the universe. A light-year, about 5.9 trillion miles, equals the distance light travels in one year. For example, the bright star Sirius is 8.7 light-years away, because it takes 8.7 years for light to travel from the star and reach us here on Earth. On the other hand, light from the Sun only takes 8.3 minutes to reach us, so the Sun is 8.3 light-minutes away. Stars in the sky can be thousands of light-years away, so the light you see there tonight actually left the star thousands of years before you were born!

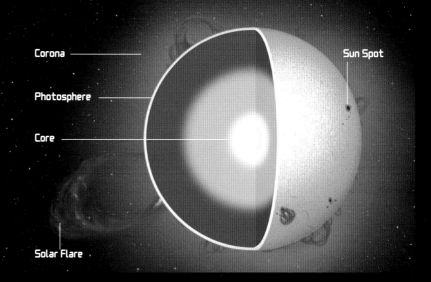

Corona

Photosphere

Core

Solar Flare

Sun Spot

THE STARS TO SCALE

Using the parking lot or basketball court of your school, your class can create a star scale. You will need:

- a 6-foot piece of string.
- a wooden dowel at least 3 feet long, or a broomstick
- measuring tape
- washable colored chalk (blue, white, yellow, orange, and red)
- notebook paper
- scissors

The stick, string, and chalk will become a giant compass with which to draw the star outlines.

For the O star, connect the blue chalk to one end of the string, unwind the string until it is 36 inches, or 3 feet long, and wrap it several times around the stick. One person should hold the stick or upside-down broomstick still, while another pulls as tightly on the string as possible, places the chalk to the ground, and walks all the way around the stick to complete a circle. Color the circle in blue.

Repeat this step for the B star, unwinding the string 18 inches, or 1.5 feet. Use the blue chalk for this as well, but when you color it in, do so a lot lighter than the O Star, because B stars are lighter blue.

Repeat again for the A star, unwinding the string 7 inches and using the white chalk.

For the F, G, and K stars, take out your paper and cut circles to use as outlines. F star (light yellow) cut a circle that is 5 inches in diameter

G star (dark yellow) cut a circle 3 inches.

K star (orange) cut a circle 1.5 inches.

M star (red) cut a circle .75 inches.

Trace each circle and color in with the corresponding color.

For a red giant star like Betelgeuse, take out your stick and string again, and make the string 65 inches, or 5.4 feet long, and make a circle using the red chalk. Bet you don't have enough chalk to color this one in!

FURTHER EXPLORATION

REAL TIME SUN IMAGES
SOHO SPACECRAFT
http://sohowww.nascom.nasa.gov/data/realtime-images.html

BIG BEAR OBSERVATORY
www.bbso.njit.edu/

NASA SITES
HUBBLE SPACE TELESCOPE
hubblesite.org/

CHANDRA X-RAY OBSERVATORY
chandra.harvard.edu/

SPITZER SPACE TELESCOPE
www.spitzer.caltech.edu/

GODDARD SPACE FLIGHT CENTER
www.nasa.gov/centers/goddard/

JPL
www.jpl.nasa.gov/

ASTRONOMY PICTURE OF THE DAY
apod.nasa.gov/apod/

EUROPEAN SPACE AGENCY
www.esa.int/SPECIALS/Education/

LAND-BASED OBSERVATORY SITES
www.cfa.harvard.edu/education/funthings.html
www.gemini.edu/

GREAT SPACE NEWS
www.skyandtelescope.com/
www.astronomy.com/
www.space.com/

BEAUTIFUL SPACE ART SITES
ASPEN SKIES/author's site
www.aspenskies.com/Aspen_Skies/Gallery.html

NOVA SPACE ART
www.novaspace.com/Gallery1.html

LYNETTE COOK
extrasolar.spaceart.org/space.html

SKY-HIGH GALLERY - Frank Hettick
www.skyhighgallery.com/

ASTRONOMY VIDEOS
www.youtube.com/results?search_query=ASTRONOMY+ANIMATIONS&search_type=&aq=f

**COOL ASTRONOMY SOFTWARE
TO MAKE YOUR OWN STARCHARTS**
VOYAGER 4.5 - Carina Software
www.carinasoft.com/

THE SKY 6 - Software Bisque
www.bisque.com/sc/pages/thesky6family.aspx

STARRY NIGHT - STARRY NIGHT STORE
www.starrynight.com/

ACKNOWLEDGMENTS

People think all you do is just sit down and write a book. Then you send it to a publisher and that's all there is to it! But, there is so much more than just that. When you read this book I want you to know there was a fantastic team of very talented people behind it. Working here at the Harvard-Smithsonian Center for Astrophysics, I had many experts to call upon when I hit a snag. I'd like to thank Dr. Mark Reid, expert on early star formation, my friends and colleagues Dr. Dimitar Sasselov and Dr. Lisa Kaltenegger for their input on the new worlds being discovered around distant stars, Dr. Johnathan McDowell, expert on black holes, Dr. Andrea Dupree, expert on high energy astrophysics, and my wonderful wife Shirley who kept the world turning while I was deeply involved with writing and painting.

My second team at National Geographic is the best this side of Alpha Centauri. I owe much to Vice President and Editor in Chief Nancy Feresten for her brilliant strokes of genius in hammering this project together, Rebecca Baines for her razor sharp editing and good cheer, and especially David Seager, Art Director, for the joy of all the brainstorming and his talent that resulted in the sheer beauty and energy of this book. Lastly, I want to acknowledge someone who passed away many years ago but still lives on in my heart. I want to thank my grandmother Mabel, a one-room country schoolteacher, algebra tutor and financial supporter of telescope making kits, science book of the month clubs, microscopes, butterfly nets, and skin diving gear. She would be so proud that all those kid's things and dreams are part of the spirit behind this book.

INDEX